Raw TAPESTRY

Poetry by:
Michael Furey

Illustrations by:
Sal Hernandez
Alice Kaminski
Rasa Joana Pojawis

Illustrations by:
Sal Hernandez: illust8r@hotmail.com
Alice Kaminski: isalicehome@yahoo.com
Rasa Joana Pojawis: pojawisr@hotmail.com

Published in Paperback 2001 by
Sarip Publishing Corp.

Designed by:
Sal Hernandez

Design Assistants:
Rasa Joana Pojawis
Michael Furey

Body text set in AGaramond

Published by Alphagraphics Toronto

Printed and bound in Canada

ISBN 1-894734-00-9

Dedication

This book is dedicated
to Mary Genevieve Bruce,
whose grace and wit
continue to enrich
the lives of all
who meet her.

R
a
w

T
a
p
e
s
t
r
y

Poetry by Michael Furey

Table of Contents

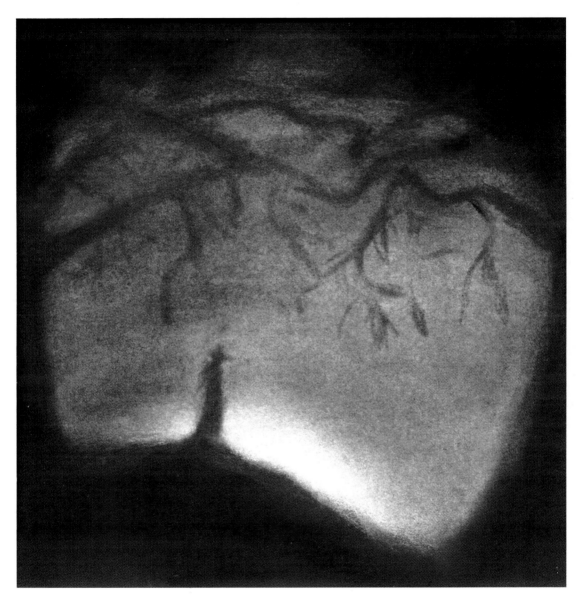

Mount Tears

What stories
have been dozed
by that shoveler's grave
deep into the bowels
of oblivion,
braving out
the monsters
of memories.

Making light
of discordant music,
shunning sharp pain,
blanching souls
of sensitivity,
scorching feelings
of coldness.

Where,
in that world
of wishes,
does the hurt heart
find its haunted home
and reach back
to that forever
forbidden past.

Standing
at the once
glorious foothills
of the Mount,
tears
from its summit
stream down
my cheeks,
the fear
no longer
finding its place
in those dark reaches
of yesterday's truths.

At its empty epicenter
of silenced sadness,
light
has now touched
life's nerve,
charging the challenge
to slow the spin
of season,
and welcome
a new day
that knows
no dusk
no dawn.

Narrow Snowflakes

Brief carefree narrow snowflakes fall,
from nimbus domes known echoes all,
espousing earth and humankind,
like feints of fire born cold refined.

Tripping lightly along their way,
uncertain whence their passions play,
toddling toward the ground unstained,
frolicking freely unrestrained.

Mounting a missive, charging truth,
burden-bound with age and youth,
sobered by surreal deference,
their homelessness their reference.

Molds much like us in simple modes,
of lucent essence water-codes,
one stubborn variance from each,
insouciance sure snowflakes teach.

A fragile mark alone one makes,
in common coil of strength partakes,
eternal barter taunting time,
eschews sin's sacredness from crime.

Tearless clouds now bittersweet,
commingled, tested under feet,
stealth silent spirits we bemoan,
reclaim forever's orphaned throne.

9

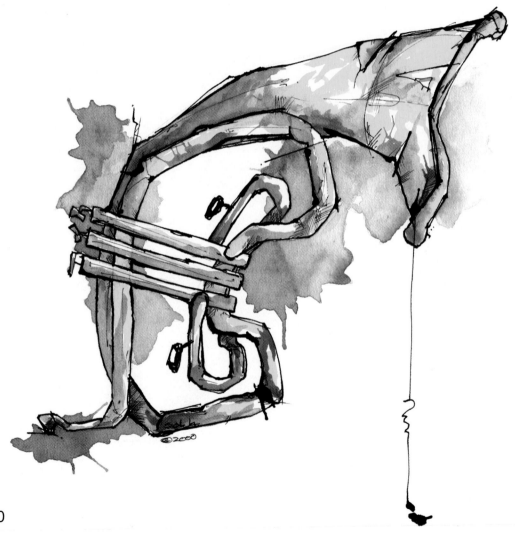

An Ode to Art

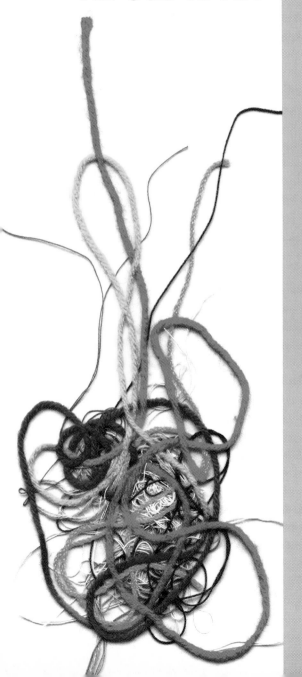

Your flugelhorn new muted now,
your flumpet won't be heard,
in be-bop classics that you scored
your spirit is preserved.

Quiet quells the *Farmer's Market*,
the *Silk Road* gems you gave,
ebbing forever in jazz land
on rhythmic soulful wave.

Freedom found its jubilant home
mid thrill-filled tunes you shared,
while hearts rollicked on every one
of all the notes you dared.

As debtors each we owe to you
a fee we'll never pay,
but you would only have it thus,
your choiceless gift to play.

In memories we will find you now
that strum up from within,
as you dazzle that *Stardust* place
of jazz-fame's honored kin.

What pleasure you'll be to angels,
their treasure home-secure,
to chorus full-stringed harps they play
in heaven new-made pure.

Bombs of Joy

At precisely 6:15 p.m. EST
joy bombed the world today
making Vesuvius and Hiroshima
resemble pompom rehearsals
for firecracker parties,
stunning the groggy
and the guarded.

You know how
your bones
can ache
with these things,
vice-gripping
flesh with spirit,
grafting reality to delusion.

Moments like these
crumble confines
of cowardice,
colour choices, creeds
and music biases
that otherwise ostracize us
in tone-deaf merriment.

Imagine the planet,
or any part of it,
where hopeless hatred
and limitless love
find conciliatory habitation;
that'd be probing
living's aorta.

12

In optional scenarios,
where planning's lacking,
there's always flights of fancy;
plans demand
solicitous preparations anyway,
while wonderlands
bounce jovially in boundlessness.

Seven coffees later,
staring at hot hands,
sweatiness clamors
'It's credible! Not phantasm!'
with that imprimatur,
who needs bishops,
verities will whim their way
past bombings.

Raw Tapestry

Purged by rare rain that night
scant caring dared a callous heart,
bound to a solo wing of flight
for an upstaged player's paltry part;

      like some heartless paramour
      you entered as you had before,
      rousing strings of love's lost grace
      stark eyes did birth yearning's grimace;

for the moment when we met
life's pathway leaned ajar,
into a tome the soul had let
you lured me from afar;

      we pine awhile and wile away
      to pine again another day,
      languid amidst Camelot trees
      we fabricate life's fantasies;

you took me to that eerie place
as if to make me pay,
the lurid loss of a lover's face
quaint coldness did betray;

      longing thus had gulled its gust
      by holding one too near,
      the saga found its broken trust
      and pained the pact with fear;

to wit the artist's part is played,
in myriad modes the fool is slayed,
to be reborn more perfectly
of wefts and weaves, raw tapestry …

For Alice

The river rushes
with as much vigor
as that first time
my heart rested
on the banks
of your
fruit-filled shore;

you stood shyly,
rapt in the 48 years
you'd graced this planet,
smiling affably
through generous portions
of all you could offer;

naïve to the depth
of your kindness,
bursting with
your mid-life needs,
our innocence met
in a place
neither of us
really knew;

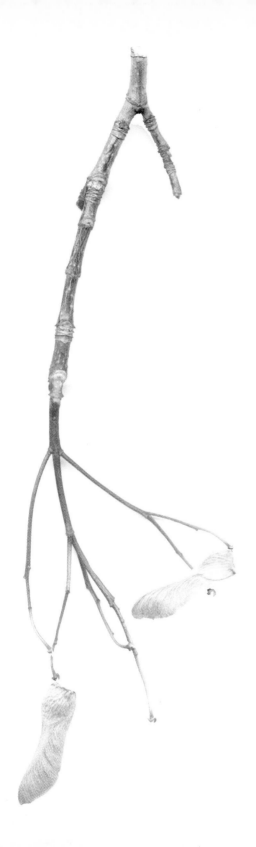

there are no reasons
to bring you back
to this mad world,
but to whisper
in your heart,
'I understand your pain',
as that anguish
is now mine too;

it's inevitable,
for time,
flaunting its mask
of late awakening,
marks us all
with the ultimate
departure from living,
in the intimacy
of loving;

how fitting
that we shared
such frivolous joy
at Westbank,
into the fading memory
of life
is the carefree cheer
of timeless youth

Signal Sunrise

Resurrected from sleep
by the early
hours of love
I sail across
the softest ocean
my eyes
have ever touched;

whales grace
the dawn air
as the sun's lip
flirts with
a shy horizon;

alone,
on this hill
of wonder,
filling the lungs
of my soul
with the air
of prayer,
entranced
by the haunting crawl
of star's
consumption
of earth;

elated,
humbled
by the mystery
of this miracle,
I slip longingly back
to the root
of my reverie's inspiration –

those heart-halting rushes
that give life
to the meaning
of eternity.

Leaves

Incarnations' verdant repose,
sun's golden accolades disclose,
breathing nourishing life on us,
with lustrous emerald deciduous.

Springing from embryonic bud,
vivacious veins plenish lifeblood,
whirling winds with raison d'être,
whisking wings with courtly gesture.

Unconscious of Spartan life spans,
nomadic air's equestrians,
tranquil lungs for folk and beasts,
sanctified omnipotent priests.

Summers' glows broadly beam,
reflecting gaiety's child-like leam,
outstretched limbs, calming seas,
subdue sorrows with arrant ease.

Colours scintillate autumn dress,
conscripting land-lift loveliness,
soils' famished paunch pleads for feed,
plants' immemorial barter-cede.

Whilst winters' pensive pallid cold,
scoops falls' gourds, as it's chronicled,
succumbing to a stark insight,
shielding youthful upright delight.

Balancing beams' fearless guess,
prizing primeval loftiness,
inverting sordid stains to graces,
effervescent leaves reign races.

Reincarnations' boundless range,
chlorophyll's victorious exchange,
nature's noble puissant ploys,
vow perennial counterpoise.

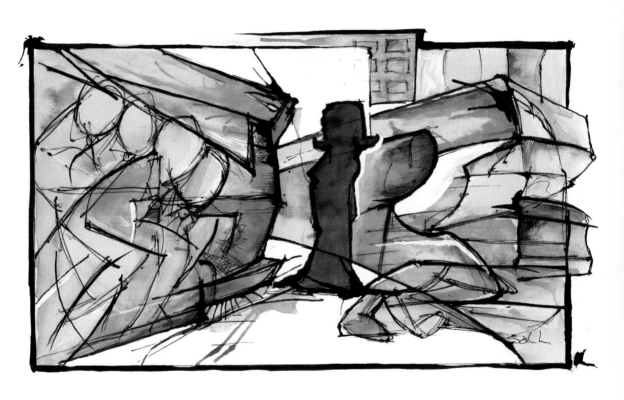

21

Bliss Avenue

Drifting down
First Avenue
one early afternoon,
I spotted
a smile
that paused
my day,
inspiring this tune.

Such things are rare
on city streets
where people
matter least,
we rush for this
and rush for that
bearing crumbs
in lieu of feast.

All at once,
through the haze
of life's hustle,
hesitance halts our souls,
inviting us
to veer toward chance
to let wonder
bliss its tolls.

We lolled and looked
at each other's face,
then coyly
at the ground,
both heads and hearts
were dizzy,
yet spun
without a sound.

'Hello', you sparred
so simply,
anointing air
with voice,
*You look
so very lovely*',
words flanked
without a choice.

The moment seemed
to last so long,
as we lingered
side by side,
that word-rich tongues
be-gift in us,
love's tension
to subside.

Such wanton treasures
rarely find
their feat
left haply unexplored,
that would-be lovers
should balance scales
of languor's
lost recórd.

Then bravely
I did walk with you,
till the corner
of our world,
the light blushed red
in the air above,
as if a beacon
in a swirl.

But you leaned left
and I to right
as we meekly
parted ways,
I knew just then
our thoughts'd merge
in flashes
of future days.

24

Blinded

Who could guess his agony,
where were the bright grief signs,
nowhere in his distance
were paths distinctly lined;

darting through a deadened daze,
light's sharpest strobe did shine,
dispelling despairing darkness
with a piquant placid find;

this delight that's been discovered,
at peril's edged incline,
is the bounty they'd almost lost
to vacuity of his crime;

romantics are vital warrants,
paladins in our clime,
pulsars' enchanted chaperons,
life-breath sprightly sublime;

how could she exonerate
his merciless disdain,
the boorish pride that buffered him
from her passion and her pain;

re-bonded as one life this day,
united in one mind,
they'll relish renewed loyalty,
beyond all text of time.

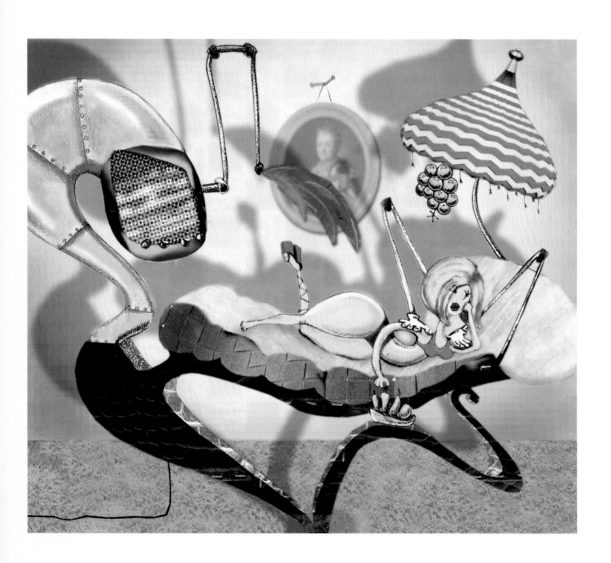

When bulls see red,
rage roars rabid,
horns hoot
for blood;
but the comic's
lungs got air
that Friday –
as he stood
some distance
from her
puttied vista,
burgundy shorts
squeezed
cellulite secrets
unabashed;

*'Why should I use
your machines',*
was her
muttered retort,
*'they only
steal jobs
from the needy;
on the other hand
they're good,
I suppose,
if they allow
more leisure hours
for people.'*

As tidy sums
of bills and coins
were tucked in
tattered clutch,
she huffed, heeled
and sped off
to share her booty
with other
machine lovers
beyond banks.

Leisure Machines

Misako

Surely the heavens stilled,
in a moment
of cosmic concord,
when life
was breathed
into Misako Sato,
gifting time
with an eminence
of elegant radiance
in that ephemeral genesis;

what scheme
had sadness charted
for the gold-brown eyes
of Misako Sato,
once buried
in the burden
of her mother's womb,
now born
of a heavy heart
in a stranger's land;

transfixed,
eyes became hands,
and through soul-touch,
braved the rapture
of our beings;

that night,
through the blur
of rich sushi,
tender tears
and rice communion,
our minds moaned –
soothing the sting
of silence
with sustenance,
sundering all boundaries
of cultural contrast;

in the slow motion
conclusion
to fate's fragile union,
reluctant hands
relinquished
consummate eyes
as our souls
unwrenched themselves,
allowing time
to mock mortality
with its quenchless lust
for finality.

Stars

Evening skies
blazed near and far,
nimble nerves
swallowed each star,
while delicate
one small life can be,
wild wonders each
of welkin are we.

Though lumens
had smoldered years ago,
moist orbs absorbed
glee's mystical glow,
engaging mirages
sky-coursing mind,
naught sequestered,
all lights past shined.

Death's strobic glares
gamboled delight,
earthlings were waltzing
at nod of night,
showy surfaces'
shimmering sleep,
fragility flickers
in blackest deep.

Illusions unloading
starlight acolytes,
reality dueling
charlatan celestites,
pillared on routes
of societal strife,
dimming hoaxed sinning,
helplessly rife.

Robed flares frazzled
festive invite,
tempered shrewd quasars
cherubs excite,
dawdling down troubadours'
musical roads,
blasé of covenants
bridled abodes.

Noumenal absence
accrues vigilance,
phenomenal presence
imbues brilliance,
poverty warmed
beneath mirrored worth,
generations to be
fast-feed gilt's dearth.

Quixotic Sleuth

I think, therefore I'm not
I dream, therefore I am
modest, my earthly lot,
joys' gifts, my epigram.

We enter with so little,
grow old for want of much,
chattels crimped committal,
drooling out of touch.

Heirship preoccupation
abducts one's wealth from self,
dashing emancipation,
drowning in pilfered pelf.

Armouring skins with greed
for onslaughts devoid of prize,
powered by chastened creed
for contact-cured demise.

Needing noises slew
people, two by two,
one by one anew
hedonic heists did woo.

Bell towers tingling toll
ring out o'er age-old land,
hearings faintly fold
save dead who understand.

Eons benumbed denial,
constricted rattled ruth,
implores each saddled trial,
liberate quixotic truth.

Moonstruck hopes fall free,
panicked pulses zapped,
sleuthing Muses' sea,
souling waves re-capped.

Apples No More

It's hard to believe
that we'd be
standing here
one day
without apples,
yet here we are
and there are
no apples anywhere.

Despite their mediation
of this whole thing
in the first place,
what?
do we just
forget about
*an apple a day
keeps the doctor away*?
or how about
*it only takes
one rotten apple
to spoil a barrel*,
are we just going
to bag that too?

Maybe we put
the wrong things
in barrels
to start with
and why
were we trying
to avoid doctors
anyhow.

Heck, there goes
the old idea
of sucking up
to the teacher
but thank God
apples were around
when the whole
Newton gravity thing
went down,
whew!
that was a lucky one!

Which kind
will you
miss most:
Granny Smiths,
Five Points,
for me
there's no
question –
nostalgic Crabapples,
I'm partial
to sour stuff.

Mist Time

The flower bloomed
before the setting
of the bud
last nite,
draping its
emptiness
near callousness,
repudiating shame,
closing its
gentleness
unscathed.

By morning,
no rain
was necessary,
teardrops drenched
the petals
of sadness.

Lamented mist time,
like unwonted flowers'
shunned readiness,
blushing unbridled,
posing utterly unaware.

Like a diligent
sentinel,
inflating veins
with revving expectation,
watching,
undeterred
by slumber,
whereupon
knowing is readied
for resolution,
on clock's
cheif clang
of chime.

38

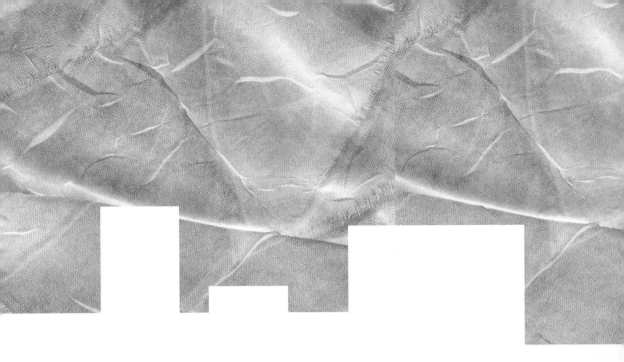

Tower Glamour

From tower glamour
her centered thought
shook footholds;
that humbling sensorial
which coolly captivates,
snapped unwittingly
in her sultry
delirious message.

How could it be possible,
that a woman
so beautiful,
engagingly merry,
busy about
world whizzing affairs
with the royal
and the rich,
would subvert
such preoccupancy
for the warmth
in her blood
that is him.

39

Answers to fussy questions
from frantic newcomers
are donned
by an inner shrill,
whose cognizance
shivers
with quiet coos
of secret-safe
sense memoirs,
miles from
her present
tested vantage.

No trained finale
can demystify
zenith zing
glazing grooves
in chalked cheeks;
lasered wrinkles
would rashly defile
scarce rhythm
released
by her energy,
committed in perpetuity
on air's
faithful vibrato.

Soul Speak

You asked me how I'd speak to you
I answered *'with my soul'*
Whence quiet classics may endue
Bodies, e'en worn and old.

Meager wordings are mannered means
In spaces lines truth par,
For spirits of their in-betweens
Host knowing who we are.

In actions we affirm much more
Than primary preaches can,
Done deeds properly reassure
Bearings of each human.

Loftier lies are wrought of eyes
Than tongues can ever tell,
Sight-vipers' clever cordial cries,
Proud progenies of hell.

Interpretations spade their spot
In kept and keenest minds,
Paled passive to a wordy lot
Both brusque and savvy kinds.

Take each venting that you're vetting
And brood them weightily,
Know probity by thus whetting
Foot-guides, lead heartily.

That heaven's gate know of your date
Dominions welcome you,
For revering through living's wait
First-affairs trepid true.

Thence fettering depths' sharpest shrew
Crass careless hopelessness,
Is guiled by good to graze anew
O'er plains' pruned openness.

41

42

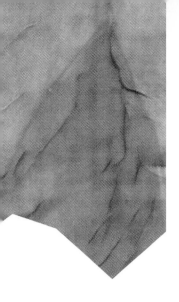

Pasture's Crown

Gazing down a country road
whose corner teased my eye,
ways of warmth and weary woes
histories its passers-by.

Glitz-icons, forebodings
entice wild wanderers' hearts,
threading veins of hills and plains
world-wards from common parts.

Star silvered sure that summer day
atop our pasture's crown,
in hay fresh cut, lazed in lees
that wine-filled air fanned down.

Touching stories we did trade,
enigmas gave way to known,
breaking still-ground in our midst,
seeding the spirit-zone.

No entries nor exits chosen,
no answers to queries posed,
laid back living on that land
where yesterday's shadows closed.

Feet floating o'er earth, we ran
freed fingers through hair, soft grass
hand-in-hand on road-slag-span
unleashed mind-borders pass.

Q-T-π

Geometrics notwithstanding,
though those measurements
by any calculation
would compute perfectly,
dazzling a didact's phiz,
deoxygenating
learned lungs of procedure,
leaving experts
of pennon threads
scrambling,
jealously camouflaging
their palpitating eagerness
to apparel her;

hall whispers
neared painfully
piercing decibels:
who is she,
where did she come from,
why is she here;
questions were consistent
with vacant stares
and stupefied silence,
as if consolidated consciousness
coveted covert closeness
with this stranger,
monotonely mystifying
carnal and sacrosanct,
with each stride
of confidence
conditions leapt without care;

then she spoke,
throngs hushed,
from finicky fiendamentalists
to rambunctious rumble-rousers
hysteria apprehended all
who quaffed
loquacious quantities
of her perceptiveness
down gaga gullets,
gorging on each
detailed deliberation;

the topic:
genetically altered foods
versus organic —
with couthie elocution
she spoke of
seedless pumpkins,
fruit without cores,
rinds falling
from oranges
at snaps of fingers,
and coconuts
laughing in trees
at blinking eyes;
keep eating your fruit
she repeated
over and over again,
in a narcotic drone
that married known
with ears on loan;

45

subconsciously relapsing
to Eden's
relished womb,
we pondered
could she be
Eve reincarnated;
are we re-witnessing
the big apple scene
on earth;
or is she the serpent
ensconced
in servile skin,
sent back
to mock and miff
Septuagintal sanctity,
reminding us
of that initial blundering
eviction notice
from Nirvana;

whatever matter may be
we think we were there,
she seems
to have been here,
and didn't our hearts burn
at the breaking into song,
while perspiring gatherings
petitioned for encore
after encore,
imploring her
to keep all metabolized,
so that humanity's
jittery juggling
of its seven fatal flaws –
inherited with fig flora –
might intensify
olympic dexterity,
until messianic reassurance
inflames that long awaited
second booting.

Internet Ravage

Havoc scowls our highways,
terror's tooting our towns,
revolts rev thoughts and spoken ways,
our world is upside down.

Mice trap us now, so it seems,
curt viruses kill for cash,
while yahoos deal boodles of screams
where meanings click to trash.

We bank and shop from couches,
take courses in our ginch,
grooving gals and guys to slouches,
this web thing is a cinch.

For con men and their gunmen
the program has them pissed,
key codes have all been broken
their wallet-walls unhitched.

Hulks had left their haunts by night
while keepers snored and slept,
life's pieces had been safe and tight
till the onslaught of this Internet.

Paid passes for mummed masses,
they're howling in their seats,
sex with reaming voyeur rashes,
Sodom-screens scroll tasty treats.

But police states don't lie lightly,
those gunners will attack,
they'll shackle controls so tightly,
fox-fence a fitter tact.

These electric pills have poisons
of euphoric irony,
their glutinous fettered foisons
hull hubbubs dullard-dizzy.

Patong Sun

On an island known to the West
for *The Man With the Golden Gun*,
we journeyed on our sacred quest
to the setting of Patong sun.

Shore air and water banded,
sleek cadence cued by two,
on wavelengths, beach stranded
nigh nude ocean's watchet blue.

Risqué tangled desires,
streaming asteroids' sparkle-works,
afloat whitecaps' flushing fires
Eastern poise schooled vagrant quirks.

Synchronizing systolic hearts,
plunging sun's gleams of gold,
every measure of earthen arts
glossing freely, fold upon fold.

Routines and rarities trimmest
sights pre nor post made known,
pliant dyadic hypnotists,
impaling groan with moan.

Mellow currents for hale did reach
all elements on wind and wave,
enveloping genteel strengths of each,
discerning sea-souls' restive conclave.

Anesthetized atop summit,
knurling clenching crackling sand,
quaking trumps' triumphant plummet,
redeeming each tanned sweat gland.

Chaste seventh heaven peace ordained
full honoured vessels' syntheses,
impeccable framed round profane,
staying planetary syzygies.